THE COLORS OF PRAYER

BIBLE STUDY GUIDE AND BIBLE MARKING PLAN

SECOND EDITION

Donna L. Bechthold

WESTBOW
PRESS®
A DIVISION OF THOMAS NELSON
& ZONDERVAN

Unless otherwise indicated, all Scripture quotations are taken from the Holy Bible, New Living Translation, copyright © 1996, 2004, 2007, 2013, 2015 by Tyndale House Foundation. Used by permission of Tyndale House Publishers, Inc., Carol Stream, Illinois 60188. All rights reserved.

Scripture quotations taken from the New American Standard Bible® (NASB), Copyright © 1960, 1962, 1963, 1968, 1971, 1972, 1973, 1975, 1977, 1995 by The Lockman Foundation. Used by permission. www.Lockman.org

Scripture marked (KJV) taken from the King James Version of the Bible.

WestBow Press books may be ordered through booksellers or by contacting:

WestBow Press
A Division of Thomas Nelson & Zondervan
1663 Liberty Drive
Bloomington, IN 47403
www.westbowpress.com
1 (866) 928-1240

Because of the dynamic nature of the Internet, any web addresses or links contained in this book may have changed since publication and may no longer be valid. The views expressed in this work are solely those of the author and do not necessarily reflect the views of the publisher, and the publisher hereby disclaims any responsibility for them.

Any people depicted in stock imagery provided by Getty Images are models, and such images are being used for illustrative purposes only. Certain stock imagery © Getty Images.

ISBN: 978-1-9736-3223-8 (sc)
ISBN: 978-1-9736-3224-5 (e)

Library of Congress Control Number: 2018907572

Print information available on the last page.

WestBow Press rev. date: 08/24/2018

DEDICATION

To my precious family:

Wayne, my husband of fifty-five years,
who at the beginning said, "You need to share this."

Chrisi, Brenda, and Deana, our lovely daughters,
and their spouses

Natasha, Chris, Nick, Amanda, Sean, Kristen, Jeff,
our grandchildren and their families

Aron, Aubree, Alyssa, Evan, Ava,
our amazing great-grandchildren

To my good friend, Madeline
I am forever grateful for
her encouragement over the years.
Thank you!

and

you, dear reader!

_____

(Your Name)

CONTENTS

PART 1

THE COLORS OF PRAYER

INTRODUCTION

Welcome to *The Colors of Prayer: A Bible Study Guide and Bible Marking Plan*. This little study guide is just a beginning. It is my prayer that the use of this guide will inspire the sincere student to seek a deeper immersion in God's Word and prayer and to experience a closer, more intimate walk with Him.

This book is based on an acrostic of the word *PRAYER*. It is simple enough for a child to understand and learn, but also complex enough that a lifetime of study will not exhaust it. *The Colors of Prayer* touches every aspect of life. It is appropriate for prayer any time, any place. It is most appropriate for private prayer.

If ever there was a time when God's children are seeking a closer walk with Him, that time is now. As we see the events taking place around us, and around our world, we sense an urgent feeling that the earth is in a downward spiral, and Jesus is soon to come.

God's Word is the Bread of Life. It speaks to us of Jesus, who gave His life for us. Scripture provides nourishment that feeds and strengthens us spiritually, mentally, and physically.

When we spend time reading and studying God's Word, a desire grows within. We desire our relationship with God and our faith in Jesus to be a growing and vital part of our lives, every day and moment by moment.

God's Word admonishes us to pray without ceasing, to be always in an attitude of prayer. Scripture includes some amazingly powerful prayers. These prayers are wonderful examples that include all the colors of prayer. It has been said that prayer is a science, based on principles. The study of a science includes ingredients, order, consistency, creativity, combinations, and results. Can the same be applied to prayer? What are the ingredients? Is there order? Is there need of consistency?

If it is your sincere desire to walk with God as Enoch did, may the study of the principles of prayer become your consuming interest.

The Colors of Prayer can be studied many different ways: as a small group study guide, as an individual study guide, and as a daily devotional. It's also meaningful as a focus for a prayer emphasis weekend seminar. In a small group setting, the first session can cover the introduction and the first chapter. The remaining chapters are each covered in one session. In a weekend seminar of three sessions, the first session covers the introduction and the Praise and Response chapters, while the second and third sessions cover Admit and Yield and Expect and Rejoice.

The Colors of Prayer is a beautiful and meaningful daily devotional resource and guide. There is a list of scripture texts at the end of each section of the study guide. One suggestion is to choose one text from each list. Write the key letters P, R, A, Y, E, R underneath each other on the left side of lined paper. Beside each letter, write the scripture and text. Use each verse for the foundation of your devotional prayer. The beauty of this is that you are using God's Word in a very personal way. Hopefully, you will soon find that you automatically reach for your Bible at prayer time. As you are drawn more and more to the Word of God, you will discover many texts to add to the lists. You will have difficulty choosing only one.

My Prayer

Let my prayer begin with **PRAISE**
as I lift my voice to Thee.
May my **RESPONSE** of thanks ascend
as I bow on bended knee.
Forgive me as I **ADMIT** and confess
and **YIELD** my will and my way.
Grant me the courage to **EXPECT** great things
as I ask and Your promises claim.
Let my every prayer conclude
with expressions of joy and love
as I **REJOICE** in abundant blessings,
flowing from your throne above.

The Prayer

P	**Praise**	Express adoration
R	**Respond**	Respond with gratitude
A	**Admit**	Admit sin, confess, repent
Y	**Yield**	Yield, surrender, obey
E	**Expect**	Ask, believe, claim promises
R	**Rejoice**	Conclude with joy

The Colors of Prayer is also a Bible marking plan. Scriptures that relate to each of these colors of prayer are found from Genesis to Revelation. Highlight them in these suggested colors: purple for verses of praise; red for verses regarding our response of thankfulness; amber or orange for verses regarding admitting our sin and asking for and accepting forgiveness; yellow for yielding and surrendering; emerald green for expecting great things as we claim God's promises; and royal blue for verses that free us to go on our way rejoicing in His goodness. These hues fill our Bible with the colors of prayer.

The Colors

P	**Purple**	Praise royalty
R	**Red**	Respond with gratitude
A	**Amber**	Admit, confess, repent
Y	**Yellow**	Yield, surrender
E	**Emerald Green**	Expect, ask, and claim
R	**Royal Blue**	Rejoice, express great joy

Let God's Word become a beautiful part of your prayer. Read the scriptures that illustrate or speak to the different aspects of your prayer. Pray God's Word back to Him.

When you put the colors of prayer and God's Word together, prayer becomes a new and refreshing experience that frees you to claim God's promises. As portions of scripture are identified to develop a dynamic prayer life; and as you highlight them with the colors, your Bible becomes filled with a rainbow of color, the colors of prayer.

The Lord's Prayer

Jesus gave us a beautiful example of prayer in the Lord's Prayer. What does this simple yet complex prayer include? Are there principles involved that I should know?

Challenges

There are many books with thousands of inspiring quotations that encourage us to become prayer warriors.

The Word of God overflows with scriptures that inspire us to seek a fervent prayer life:

"I love all who love me, those who search will surely find me" (Proverbs 8:17).

"The Lord has heard my plea, the Lord will answer my prayer" (Psalm 6:9).

"My eyes will be open and My ears attentive to every prayer made in this place" (2 Chronicles 7:15).

"But God did listen! He paid attention to my prayer" (Psalm 66:19).

"Take delight in the Lord, and he will give you your heart's desires" (Psalm 37:4).

But What about James 4:3?

"You ask and do not receive, because you ask with wrong motives, so that you may spend it on your pleasures" (NASB).

"And even when you ask, you don't get it because your motives are all wrong—you want only what will give you pleasure." (NLT)

What does it mean to ask with "wrong motives"?

_____

_____

What Is Prayer?

There are many answers:

- Prayer is a science; there are principles.
- Prayer is a sense of God's presence.
- Prayer is unlimited joy and power.
- Prayer is communion with God.
- Prayer is opening the heart to God.
- Prayer is dialogue: talking and listening.
- Prayer is a habit with me.
- Prayer is life to my soul.
- Prayer is "good news."
- Prayer is laying my concerns before Him.

What is your answer? What is prayer to you?

_____

_____

O Lord, I cry out to you. I will keep on pleading day by day.

—Psalm 88:13

The Golden Hour

In trauma care, there is a critical period of time called the "golden hour." If the victim of a severe trauma receives appropriate medical attention within that first hour, the chances of survival are greatly increased. The victim is sometimes spoken of as being salvageable versus nonsalvageable. So it is with us; we have a critical need to meet with God during that golden hour, that first hour of the day. The golden hour of prayer can make all the difference, and the difference may mean our survival.

My Commitment

_____

_____

_____

_____

_____

_____

_____

This is not a book that you will read once and put on the shelf. You will find yourself returning to it over and over through the years, as it contains the beauty of the gospel message in its pages. As you continue to read and study scripture, you will identify hundreds of verses that will become a part of your prayer life.

Before You Begin

Compare different versions and translations. One Bible may use the word *praise*, while another, in the same verse uses *thanks*. Let your Bible speak to your heart.

Some verses will include more than one color of prayer. Select the major theme and highlight with that color. You may choose to add the second color by placing a dot or small circle of the second color in the margin.

As you complete *The Colors of Prayer*, you will find God's life-giving messages easily identified, settled in your heart, simple to find, and easy to share.

Read one color from Genesis to Revelation and experience the blessing of God's message of salvation throughout scripture. You will be amazed. Your Bible will come alive.

I recommend Crayola pencil crayons because they have a soft lead; they don't leak through, and I have found them to work very well for even the most delicate paper.

It is my prayer that you will find *The Colors of Prayer Bible Marking and Study Plan* to be a source of joy to your heart as you experience the richness of making God's Word a vibrant part of your prayer life.

PRAYER

CHAPTER 1

Praise

Purple

Express Adoration

We often begin our prayers with "I praise You for ..." without really thinking about what we are saying.

The scriptures instruct us over and over again to praise God. Praise Him for His creative powers, sustaining powers, redemptive powers. Praise Him for who He is: the great and awesome God. It's easy to praise Him when all is going well, when we feel good. But there are times when life seems bleak. We don't feel good physically, emotionally, or spiritually. Here we find the first principle of prayer: It doesn't matter what's happening in our lives; it does not change who God is. He is still the mighty majesty, the one who has made all things and is upholding all life in His hands. He is the only one who can be trusted to not change, no matter what.

Praise Sets the Stage

Let's not approach God with a list of our needs, desires, and concerns without contemplating who He is. How do we reconcile the awesome majesty of the Creator and sustainer of the universe with the endearing title of Father?

This is one of the mysteries of scripture that will ever challenge our faith: to know, beyond a doubt, that the great God of eternity cares about me, individually, on this little speck of a planet.

There is only one place to satisfy this dual role, and that is in the scriptures themselves. It is almost impossible to bring joy into our prayer life unless we spend time in God's Word. And so if we would praise God, we must search the scriptures and find for ourselves the reason for praise. We must discover, for ourselves, who He is and what He is like.

Central to our focus on praise is acknowledgment of God as Creator and sustainer of life. The first five words of the Bible declare God as Creator: "In the beginning God created ...." The scriptures go on to tell us that what He created was good, and when He completed His work of creation, He rested and provided a memorial for us, whereby we may praise Him.

What Is Praise?

What words come to mind when you think of praise as it relates to God? My favorite is *adoration*.

_____

_____

When we praise, we recognize and acknowledge who God is: Creator, Savior, redeemer, protector. The more we are aware of the majesty of the one we worship, the more we will praise, and the more we will hold God in reverence.

The Lord's Prayer

Jesus gave us an example of praise as He approached the Father's throne in prayer: "Our Father, which art in heaven, Hallowed be Thy name" (Matthew 6:9 KJV).

Jesus recognized and acknowledged God's place in the universe and the holiness of His name. He approached His Father with all the faith and trust a small child feels when approaching his earthly father. We may do the same toward our heavenly Father.

> The people whom I formed for Myself will declare My Praise.
> —Isaiah 43:21 (NASB)

> Let them Praise your great and awesome name, your name is holy.
> —Psalm 99:3

As you read the following verses, ask yourself, Who is this God? What is He like?

What Does the Bible Say?

ABOUT GOD'S NAME

Why is God's name important?

Psalm 48:10 _____

What descriptive terms do the scriptures apply to God?

WHO IS HE?

Job 37:23 _____

Psalm 8:1 _____

Job 37:22 _____

Isaiah 33:21 _____

Isaiah 6:1 _____

Daniel 2:47_____

Isaiah 9:6 _____

Isaiah 64:8 _____

Isaiah 6:3 _____

ABOUT GOD'S ATTRIBUTES

What characteristics do the scriptures apply to God?

WHAT IS HE LIKE?

Psalm 115:1_____

Psalm 29:1, 2 _____

Job 36:4 _____

Job 12:13 _____

Nehemiah 9:31_____

Deuteronomy 32:3, 4_____

Job 36:5 _____

Nehemiah 4:14 _____

WHEN DO WE PRAISE?

Psalm 113:3 _____

Psalm 145:2 _____

Psalm 34:1 _____

WHY DO WE PRAISE?

Job 33:4 _____

Isaiah 52:7 _____

HOW DO WE PRAISE?

1 Chronicles 16:9 _____

2 Chronicles 7:6 _____

WHAT IS THE SOURCE OF OUR PRAISE?

Psalm 40:3 _____

There are many examples of praise in prayer in scripture. How do some of these great prayers include praise?

2 Kings 19:15 _____

Nehemiah 1:5 _____

1 Chronicles 29:10–13 _____

2 Chronicles 6:14 _____

2 Chronicles 20:6 _____

Oh Father, give me a sense of who You are.
Help me recognize Your majesty and power.
Help me to see that, come what may,
You are who You are—the same every day.

WHAT DOES PRAISE MEAN TO ME?

_____

_____

My Personal Praise

_____

As you continue your quest for additional examples of praise, look for verses that include the following phrases: "Almighty," "exalted," "majestic," "awesome," "holy," "Creator," "compassionate," "lovingkindness," "gracious," and "merciful."

There are over twelve hundred verses in scripture telling us to praise; they describe who He is and what He is like. Spend time in scripture contemplating who He is, identifying those verses that speak to praise. Let praise be an essential part of your prayer.

Praise Texts

- Genesis 1:1
- Deuteronomy 10:21
- Judges 5:3
- 1 Samuel 2:2, 3
- 2 Samuel 7:22
- 1 Kings 8:23
- 1 Chronicles 16:12
- Ezra 3:11
- Nehemiah 1:5
- Job 9:4
- Job 10:12
- Job 37–40
- Psalm 3:3
- Psalm 11:4
- Psalm 18:1
- Psalm 21:13
- Psalm 30:12
- Psalm 40:5

- Isaiah 12:5
- Isaiah 42:10
- Jeremiah 17:14
- Lamentations 3:22, 23
- Ezekiel 34:31
- Daniel 2:20, 23
- Daniel 4:3
- Joel 2:26
- Amos 4:13
- Luke 10:21
- Romans 11:34
- Ephesians 5:19
- Philippians 2:9–11
- James 5:13
- 1 Peter 1:7
- Revelation 4:8
- Revelation 5:12

P̃RAYER   R̃

CHAPTER 2

Respond

Red

Express Gratitude and Thanks

Praising God prompts a spontaneous Response of gratitude and thankfulness. One can't help but thank Him for who He is and what He has done, and is doing, for us.

> Thou art my God, and I give thanks to Thee.
> Thou art my God, I extol Thee.
> —Psalm 118:28 (NASB)

Donna L. Bechthold

What Is Gratitude? What Is Thankfulness?

What words come to mind as you think of gratitude and thankfulness, as they relate to giving thanks to God? What does thankfulness feel like?

The Lord's Prayer

> For Thine is the kingdom, and the power, and the glory forever.
> —Matthew 6:13 (KJV)

Many authors assign praise and thanksgiving to this passage of the Lord's Prayer. Jesus did not conclude His prayer with a doubtful attitude but in full faith that He had been heard. He left the matter with God and gave thanks for the answers that were sure to come.

> I will give you thanks, O Lord, with all my heart.
> —Psalm 138:1

The Mature Emotion

Gratitude has been called the "mature emotion." Little children show their delight with a gift, but they do not have the understanding that enables them to appreciate the value of the time and money spent. They are not yet grown-up. As children grow into adulthood, they begin to have a sense of what had to take place for the gift to become a reality.

That is the question we can ask ourselves. Do we have an understanding of the value of the gifts we receive from God? Do we recognize the treasure in the simple things of life: a child's hug, fertile soil, golden sunsets, a warm bed, a hot meal, clean clothes? In addition, do we recognize the treasure in the profound things of life (the gift of Jesus, eternal life) and so much more?

We can imagine a gift room in heaven, with our name over the door. As we walk in, we see many beautifully wrapped gifts, and then we look at the labels. We see many gifts that God had prepared for us while we lived on this earth, gifts that could have been ours if only we had asked. I want my gift room in heaven to be empty. I don't want anything to be in there that I could have had today.

What Does the Bible Say?

WHAT IS AN ESSENTIAL COMPONENT OF PRAYER?

Philippians 4:6 _____

Colossians 4:2 _____

WHAT GIFTS ARE OFFERED BY GOD?

Ecclesiastes 3:13 _____

Acts 2:38 _____

Romans 5:17 _____

Romans 5:18 (KJV) _____

Ephesians 2:8, 9 _____

Ephesians 4:7 _____

> Every good thing bestowed and every perfect gift is
> from above, coming down from the Father of lights, with
> Whom there is no variation, or shifting shadow.
> —James 1:17 (NASB)

Have I claimed these gifts as my own? _____

Donna L. Bechthold

WHY CAN I BE THANKFUL?

Psalm 139:14 _____

Psalm 86:15 _____

Revelation 3:20 _____

James 5:11 _____

2 Peter 3:9 _____

1 Timothy 1:15 _____

1 Chronicles 16:34 _____

Isaiah 25:1 _____

Psalm 118:21 _____

1 Corinthians 15:57 _____

Revelation 21:4 _____

Philippians 4:19 _____

Romans 5:8 _____

Acts 2:21 _____

Romans 8:34 _____

Acts 1:11_____

HOW CAN I BE THANKFUL?

1 Chronicles 16:8 _____

Psalm 26:7 _____

Psalm 147:7 _____

Daniel 6:10 _____

WHEN CAN I BE THANKFUL?

Psalm 30:12 _____

Psalm 79:13 _____

Ephesians 5:20 _____

1 Thessalonians 5:18 _____

Does my gratitude come from a mature heart? Do I understand the value of God's gifts?

My Personal Response of Thanks and Gratitude

_____

_____

_____

_____

_____

As you continue your quest for additional examples of Respond, look for verses with the following phrases: "give thanks," "thanksgiving," "offer," "gift," and "gratitude."

Respond Texts

- 2 Samuel 22:50
- 1 Chronicles 16:8
- Psalm 18:49
- Psalm 26:7
- Psalm 30:4
- Psalm 30:12
- Psalm 35:18

- Psalm 75:1
- Psalm 79:13
- Psalm 100:4
- Psalm 105:1
- Psalm 136
- Psalm 140:13
- Daniel 6:10

- Jonah 2:9
- 2 Corinthians 4:15
- 2 Corinthians 9:11, 15
- Ephesians 5:4
- Ephesians 5:20
- Hebrews 13:15

CHAPTER 3

CHAPTER 3

Admit

Amber (Orange)

Forgive, Confess, and Repent

The kindness of God leads you to repentance.
—Romans 2:4 (NASB)

Admitting guilt is not easy. Apologizing is not easy. Repenting is not easy. It's easy to say, "Please forgive my many sins." But admitting is more than saying a few words; it means honesty: honesty with God, honesty with yourself, and honesty with others.

Honesty with God

There is nothing in your life He does not already know, nothing you cannot bring to Him. He knows what tempts you, He knows your weaknesses, He knows what is going on inside. He knows your past, your present, and your future. Talk with Him.

Honesty with God includes considering our use of time, money, and talents; asking forgiveness for when we have wasted them; and then consecrating those energies for His plan and to His glory.

> Then hear Thou in heaven Thy dwelling place, and forgive and act
> and render to each according to all his ways, whose heart Thou
> knowest, for Thou alone dost know the Hearts of all the sons of men.
> —1 Kings 8:39 (NASB)

Honesty with Yourself

This is a difficult topic. You must be honest with yourself in order to be honest with God, and vice versa. Honesty with yourself means facing yourself as you and God know you, as you really are. Being honest with yourself means looking inside, acknowledging all that you see, the good and the not-so-good. Honesty with yourself leads you to deal with those issues, maybe for the first time.

Honesty with oneself includes looking at old hurts, resentments, anger, and bitterness. Many times, we appear to be healthy on the outside, while inside a battle is raging. It is really critical for our physical, emotional, and spiritual health that these old things be allowed to pass away. When we hold on to these old scars, we are cheating ourselves out of everything joyous that God has planned for us.

> Get rid of all bitterness, rage, anger, harsh words, and
> slander, as well as all types of evil behavior.
> —Ephesians 4:31

MBF List

Mothers and fathers must be forgiven. Sons and daughters must be forgiven. Husbands and wives must be forgiven. Ex-husbands and ex-wives must be forgiven. Your spouse's ex must be forgiven. In-laws must be forgiven. Friends must be forgiven. Enemies must be forgiven. Those who hurt you in your long-ago past must be forgiven. Some you need to forgive may have already died, but you need to free your heart and forgive.

It may be you are the one you need to forgive. Honesty with yourself is not pain free, but the healing gives life. Could this be one of the greatest barriers to answered prayer: an unforgiving heart? You alone, with God's help, know who belongs on your Must Be Forgiven (MBF) list. This may be the most important list you will ever make. If you've never been one before, it's time to be a list-maker.

Honesty with Others

Honesty with others includes humanity in general, as well as other individuals. How are we treating other people, the poor, the homeless, those we label as ungodly? How are we treating others closer to us: our coworkers, friends, and family? What do we have to confess: murder, adultery, dishonesty? Maybe, but probably not. But what about indifference, unkindness, an unpleasant disposition, and selfishness?

Honesty with others includes recognizing our lack of love, confessing it, repenting, and, with the help of the Holy Spirit, changing. It is so easy to see the sins of others, but so difficult to see our own.

Sinning Right

My mother was relaxing one afternoon when a friend dropped in. They lived in a retirement center, and dropping in was fairly common. This particular afternoon, the friend sat down and began criticizing a mutual acquaintance. After she left, my mom wrote the following poem.

Sinning Right

If you don't sin like I sin,
then you're not sinning right.
I don't think you're trying
or by now you'd see the light.
I keep a very close eye on you.
I watch you with all my might,
but if you don't sin like I sin,
then you're not sinning right.

I know the scriptures tell us
that we're all sinners hcrc.
Not one of us is perfect,
the Bible makes it clear.
But I think the way I'm sinning
looks better in my sight.
So if you don't sin like I sin,
then you're not sinning right.

(Myrtle Blize © 1991)

The Spider

I love the following old story about a little old lady at prayer meeting. Week after week, she would pray and ask God to remove the cobwebs of sin from her life. This went on week after week, the same request: "Remove the cobwebs of sin from my life." Finally, a young woman was tired of hearing this, and she added her request to the old lady's prayer: "Please, God, kill the spider."

The Lord's Prayer

Jesus gave us the example of forgiveness: forgiveness from God and our forgiveness to others.

> And forgive us our debts as we forgive our debtors.
> —Matthew 6:12 (KJV)

Jesus didn't only tell us to forgive; He showed us how, on the cross.

> Jesus said, "Father, forgive them, for they don't know what they are doing."
> —Luke 23:34

What Does the Bible Say?

WHAT IS THE PROBLEM OF SIN?

Romans 5:12 _____

1 Corinthians 15:56 _____

1 John 3:4 _____

Romans 3:23 _____

WHAT IS THE PENALTY FOR SIN?

Romans 6:23 _____

WHAT IS THE PAYMENT FOR SIN?

1 Corinthians 15:3 _____

1 Peter 2:24 _____

1 John 1:7 _____

Hebrews 9:28 _____

Ephesians 1:7 _____

1 John 4:10 _____

Hebrews 10:12 _____

WHAT IS THE PROVISION FOR SIN?

Psalm 94:18 _____

Hebrews 2:18 _____

1 John 2:1 _____

1 John 5:5 _____

Matthew 26:41 _____

Psalm 119:11 _____

Romans 6:11 _____

Romans 6:14 _____

Romans 6:23 _____

WHAT IS THE PARDON FOR SIN?

Isaiah 43:25 _____

Psalm 86:5 _____

Psalm 51:7 _____

Isaiah 1:18 _____

1 John 1:9 _____

Isaiah 44:22 _____

Psalm 51:10 _____

Psalm 32:5 _____

Isaiah 55:7 _____

WHEN DO WE ADMIT OUR SIN?

Matthew 5:23, 24 _____

Matthew 18:21, 22 _____

Mark 11:25 _____

WHY DO WE ADMIT OUR SIN?

Romans 4:7, 8 _____

Luke 15:7, 10 _____

Hebrews 8:12 _____

Donna L. Bechthold

HOW DO WE ADMIT OUR SIN?

Psalm 38:18 _____

Acts 10:43 _____

1 John 1:9 _____

For Me

I think about Jesus willingly taking on all the
guilt of all the sins
of every person who has ever lived, is living, or will live,
and feeling the awful separation from God that sin causes.
I cannot comprehend how terrible it must have been.
Multiply the despair we feel when our own sin
separates us from God.
What must it have been to have carried the
guilt of all sin?
And Jesus felt that guilt.
Jesus felt that separation from God.
Yet, He willingly went to the cross,
to die for you, to die for me.
I cannot fathom such love.

There Was Love

Before Jesus came to redeem us,
there was love, there was love.
Before there was sin and suffering,
there was love, there was love.
When Jesus died on the cross to save us,
it was love, it was love.
We may not understand it,
but it's there, always there.
There was love.

(Wayne Bechthold © 1991)

As you continue your quest for additional examples of admit, look for verses with the following phrases: "forgive," "confess", "repent," "righteousness," "Calvary," "death of Jesus," "resurrection," "blood of Jesus," "offered," "sacrifice," "white as snow," "wipes out our transgressions," "a clean heart," "iniquity," and "guilt." There are over two thousand verses in scripture that talk about this amazing love.

Admit Texts

- Numbers 14:18
- 1 Kings 8:50
- 2 Chronicles 6:21
- 2 Chronicles 6:26, 27
- Ezra 10:11
- Nehemiah 1:6
- Nehemiah 9:17
- Job 14:17
- Psalm 25:11
- Psalm 25:18
- Psalm 32:1
- Psalm 79:9
- Psalm 119:133
- Isaiah 6:7
- Jeremiah 31:34
- Jeremiah 33:8
- Ezekiel 18:22
- Ezekiel 36:25
- Hosea 14:2
- Matthew 3:8
- Mark 11:25
- Luke 15:7
- John 8:11
- Acts 3:19
- Romans 4:7, 8
- 1 Corinthians 16:14
- 2 Corinthians 7:9, 10
- Galatians 5:14
- Ephesians 4:32
- Philippians 2:3, 4
- Colossians 3:13
- Hebrews 8:12
- Hebrews 10:17
- James 5:16

 PRA**Y**ER

CHAPTER 4

Yield

Yellow

Surrender and Obey

What Does It Mean to Yield?

What words, in addition to *surrender*, come to mind as you think of yielding to our heavenly Father?

_____

_____

_____

_____

_____

The Lord's Prayer

Once again, we have the beautiful example of Jesus:

> Thy kingdom come, Thy will be done in earth, as it is in heaven.
> —Matthew 6:10 (KJV)

He shows absolute surrender, total submission, perfect trust, unconditional obedience, complete yielding.

Abdicating the Throne

When earthly rulers give up their thrones, I would imagine they do so to someone with qualifications, someone qualified to rule the kingdom, who knows the people, understands the culture, and is capable of making wise decisions, someone who has the best interest of the people at heart. We can do the same. We can abdicate the throne of our lives. We can give ourselves over to someone who is better qualified than we are, someone who knows us, who is capable of making wise decisions, and who has our best interest at heart.

Submitting, surrendering, or yielding is easy to do in generalizations: "I give myself to You today." It is also easy to then go our own way. If we are specific as we surrender, it is much more difficult to take the reins back into our own hands.

What Do We Have to Yield?

We have:

Time			
Desires	Talents	Decisions	Our words
Thoughts	Interests	Goals	Family
Situations	Relationships	Plans	Our work
Appetites	Our will	Energy	
Our witness	Aspirations	Money	

Anything can happen when we are specific as we yield. We become a gift to Jesus, wrapped up, but empty. He fills us, according to His plan for us for that day. I recall a good friend telling me how she came to the place where she changed her prayer from "Please be with me today" to "Please use me in Your plan for today," and she was amazed at the difference it made in her life.

Yielding is an all-or-nothing transaction. We cannot be partially yielded. Either He has control, or we have control. Yielding is not a once-and-for-all transaction. We may reclaim the throne at any time; it is a day-by-day, moment-by-moment surrender.

The choice is ours.

> Choose today whom you will serve.... As for me
> and my family, we will serve the Lord.
> —Joshua 24:15

Three Votes

> Always remember there are three votes for your allegiance:
> God's vote,
> Satan's vote,
> and
> your vote.
> You break the tie!

Yielding and Obedience

Each new day, we choose (hopefully) to obey the laws of the land. That choice keeps us free and allows us to enjoy the privileges of citizenship. Submitting to a more qualified ruler is of benefit only when we are obedient. Yielding and obedience go hand in hand. You cannot have one without the other.

Jesus was asked which commandment was the most important:

> "The most important commandment is this: 'Listen, O Israel! The Lord our God is the one and only God. And you must love the Lord your God with all your heart, all your soul, all your mind, and all your strength. The second is equally important. Love your neighbor as yourself. No other commandment is greater than these.'" (Mark 12:28–31)

What Does the Bible Say?

WHAT ABOUT OBEDIENCE?

Psalm 40:8 _____

Matthew 19:17 _____

John 14:15 _____

GOD'S PART

What Will God Do?

Isaiah 43:1 _____

Proverbs 1:23 _____

Psalm 139:23, 24 _____

Psalm 143:10 _____

Psalm 119:105 _____

Proverbs 19:21_____

Proverbs 16:9 _____

Jeremiah 29:11 _____

Ezekiel 20:41 _____

Isaiah 58:11 _____

Isaiah 30:21 _____

Psalm 25:12 _____

Psalm 86:11 _____

Psalm 51:12 _____

Hebrews 10:36 _____

Psalm 32:8 _____

MY PART

What Can I Do?

Job 22:22 _____

Psalm 143:8 _____

Proverbs 3:5, 6 _____

Proverbs 23:26 _____

Proverbs 16:3 _____

Zechariah 13:9 _____

Matthew 4:19, 20 _____

Matthew 6:33 _____

Donna L. Bechthold

Mark 8:34 _____

Jeremiah 11:20 _____

Isaiah 45:22_____

> The eyes of the Lord search the whole earth in order to
> strengthen those whose hearts are fully committed to Him.
> —2 Chronicles 16:9

WHEN DO WE YIELD?

Psalm 25:5_____

Psalm 52:8 _____

Hosea 12:6 _____

WHY DO WE YIELD?

Psalm 16:11 _____

Job 23:14 _____

Psalm 119:165_____

Psalm 147:11 _____

HOW DO WE YIELD?

Ezra 9:5 _____

Job 23:12_____

Psalm 25:1 _____

Psalm 27:14 _____

> This is what the Lord says: "Stop at the crossroads and
> look around. Ask for the old, godly way, and walk in it.
> Travel its path, and you will find rest for your souls."
> —Jeremiah 6:16

There are over two hundred verses in scripture that refer to the action of yielding. Look for phrases that include the following: "walk in His way," "return to the Lord," "commit your way," "hope in the Lord," "they will be My people," "follow Me," "keep My commandments," "submit therefore to God," "take My yoke upon you," "give Me your heart." Other significant phrases include "surrender," "obedience," "will," "submission," "yield," "wear My yoke," "return to the Lord," "wait for the Lord," and "give Me your heart."

Yield Texts

- 1 Samuel 12:23
- 1 Kings 8:58
- 1 Chronicles 28:9
- 2 Chronicles 15:2
- Ezra 9:5
- Nehemiah 1:9
- Psalm 3:5
- Psalm 5:8
- Psalm 16:1
- Psalm 16:11
- Psalm 25:1
- Psalm 101:3
- Psalm 119:44
- Proverbs 1:33
- Ecclesiastes 8:12
- Isaiah 12:2
- Isaiah 28:23
- Isaiah 55:6
- Jeremiah 12:3
- Jeremiah 17:7
- Jeremiah 31:33
- Ezekiel 34:11
- Hosea 10:12
- Joel 2:12, 13
- Nahum 1:7
- Malachi 3:7, 16
- Matthew 6:31, 32
- Mark 10:21
- Luke 14:27
- John 5:30
- Acts 5:32
- Romans 8:28
- Ephesians 5:10
- Hebrews 11:6`

Expect

Emerald Green

Ask, Believe, Claim

Ask me and I will tell you remarkable secrets
you do not know about things to come.
—Jeremiah 33:3

What Does It Mean to "Expect"?

What words do you think of when you think of expecting great things
from God?

_____

The scriptures tell us to ask of God, anticipate, and eagerly watch for the
answer.

I will answer them before they even call to me. While they are still talking about their needs, I will go ahead and answer their prayers!

—Isaiah 65:24

Ask, and it shall be given to you; seek, and ye shall find; knock, and it shall be opened to you. For everyone who asks receives; and he who seeks finds; and to him who knocks it shall be opened.

—Matthew 7:7, 8 (NASB)

The Lord's Prayer

Give us this day our daily bread.

—Matthew 6:11 (KJV)

Jesus gave us the example of bringing our concerns and requests—for our daily needs, our spiritual well-being—to God and waiting for the answer, with assurance.

If You Can

What do you mean, "If I can"? Jesus asked.
Anything is possible if a person believes.

—Mark 9:23

Mark 9:17–25 tells the story of a father bringing his son to Jesus for healing. The father says, "Have mercy on us and help us, if You can." Jesus answered, "What do you mean, 'If I can'?" Jesus is saying, 'There's no question as to whether or not I can; the question is whether you can, whether you can believe." He says, "All things are possible to him who believes." This verse is true for us today: All things are possible, if we believe, if we have faith. This was Jesus's frequent response to those who brought their requests to Him.

Because of your faith it will happen.

—Matthew 9:29

Go back home. Because you believed, it has happened.

—Matthew 8:13

What about Faith?

Hebrews 10:22 _____

Romans 12:3 _____

1 Corinthians 2:5 _____

Matthew 21:22 _____

So faith comes from hearing, that is, hearing the
Good News about Jesus.
—Romans 10:17

Examples of Faith

Read Joshua 3:5. What could the Israelites expect?

_____

Read Joshua 3:13–17. What was required of the people?

_____

The children of Israel had come to an impossible situation. After forty years of wandering, they were on the edge of the Promised Land. The Jordan River was in flood stage from the spring rains, and it was impossible to cross over. But God gave them specific instructions: move forward! And they did. They took the first step with nothing but a flood plain before them and God's promises behind them. And God provided a clear, dry path. They did not stand and wait for the miracle to take place. They had the courage to take the first step and expect great things from God.

Read 2 Kings 5:1–14. It is the story of Naaman. The miracle occurs only after Naaman, by faith, obeys the instruction from the prophet of God.

God's Promises

There are said to be 3,573 promises or clusters of promises in God's Word. That's one promise every day for almost ten years; could they all possibly be for me?

> For by these He has granted to us His precious and magnificent promises, in order that by them you might become partakers of the divine nature, having escaped the corruption that is in the world by lust.
> —2 Peter 1:4 (NASB)

What are the conditions? Look back through *The Colors of Prayer*. Praising: acknowledging who God is. Responding: giving thanks for all He has done for you. Admitting: forgiving, confessing, and repenting, being honest with God, yourself, and others. Yielding: submitting your will and obeying His word.

What Has God Promised?

Pardon for sin, a Christ-like character, wisdom, strength to do His will, our daily needs, protection in danger, courage, understanding in daily work, understanding in spiritual things, intelligence, tact, skill, the in-dwelling Holy Spirit, and so much more: 3,560 more.

What Does the Bible Say?

HOW MAY WE APPROACH GOD?

Psalm 5:3 _____

1 Chronicles 17:25, 26 _____

Job 5:8, 9 _____

Micah 7:7 _____

1 John 5:14 _____

Hebrews 4:16 _____

Psalm 10:17 _____

Psalm 22:5 _____

Psalm 34:17 _____

Psalm 145:18_____

HOW ABLE IS GOD?

Jeremiah 32:17 _____

Job 9:10 _____

Job 42:2 _____

Numbers 11:23 _____

1 Samuel 12:16 _____

Luke 18:27 _____

Luke 1:37 _____

Hebrews 6:18 _____

HOW WILLING IS GOD?

2 Chronicles 7:15 _____

2 Chronicles 25:9 _____

Psalm 21:2 _____

Isaiah 58:9_____

Isaiah 62:4 _____

Matthew 6:8_____

Matthew 15:28 _____

Mark 10:51_____

John 14:13 _____

Romans 8:32 _____

Our God is able. What a mighty God. Our God is willing. What a loving Father.

WHEN CAN WE EXPECT?

Psalm 107:6 _____

Psalm 62:8 _____

Daniel 10:12 _____

WHY CAN WE EXPECT?

Jeremiah 17:7_____

Philippians 4:19 _____

Ephesians 3:20 _____

Romans 4:21 _____

HOW CAN WE EXPECT?

Mark 11:24 _____

Matthew 18:19, 20 _____

Jeremiah 29:12 _____

Proverbs 3:5, 6_____

> And if we know that He hears us in whatever we ask, we know
> that we have the requests which we have asked from Him.
> —1 John 5:15 (NASB)

> Therefore I say to you, all things for which you pray and ask, believe
> that you have received them, and they shall be granted you.
> —Mark 11:24 (NASB)

> And this is the promise which He made to us: eternal life.
> —1 John 2:25 (NASB)

> These things I have written to you who believe in the name of the
> Son of God, in order that you may know that you have eternal life.
> —1 John 5:13 (NASB)

Donna L. Bechthold

Needs versus Desires

Is there is a difference between needs and desires?

Read Matthew 6:25–34.

What are your needs? (verse 33)

_____

_____

When do you have these needs? (verse 34) _____

Could these be your desires for others? _____

Could These Be Some of Your Needs Today?

>   To be filled with the Holy Spirit
>   To have a hunger and thirst for spiritual things
>   To understand spiritual things
>   To have the mind and character of Jesus
>   To have a pleasant disposition
>   To fulfill God's purpose for you
>   To have intelligence, knowledge, and wisdom
>   To have a forgiving spirit
>   To practice (be aware of) the presence of Jesus
>   To use your talents for Jesus
>   To have the grace of Jesus
>   To have protection from harm
>   To have the strength to resist temptation
>   To care for your body
>   To be a better witness
>   To be a better friend
>   To be a better wife, husband, mother, father, son, daughter, grandmother, grandfather

The needs you have for yourself may be the desire or longing you have for others.

My Concerns/Requests

Jesus is asking: "What do you want me to do for you?" (Mark 10:51).

_____

_____

_____

_____

_____

Asking the Hard Questions

Will God answer our prayers just the way we want? What do we do when our prayers don't seem to be answered? How do we respond when God seems to say, "No," or "Wait, not now"? How do we have a joyful heart when we are worried about a situation that doesn't seem to be getting any better, no matter how hard we pray? Can we have joy when we seem to be waiting and waiting?

You might find the Three Js and Three Bs a source of increased trust, peace, and joy.

The Three Js: Jacob, Jericho, and Jehoshaphat.
The Three Bs: Blessings, Barriers, and Battles

In Genesis 32:26, Jacob found himself wrestling with the Lord, all night long. What did Jacob say? "I will not let you go until you bless me" (NLT).

Read Joshua chapter 6. This is the story of the children of Israel and the fall of Jericho. What did the Israelites do? They did what God told them to do. Strange as it seems, they marched around the city, voices quiet and trumpets sounding, once each day, for six days. On the seventh day, following God's instructions, they marched around the city seven times—again with voices quiet—until they were given the command to blow their trumpets and shout. And shout they did. And the walls of the city, huge barriers, came tumbling down.

You will find the story of Jehoshaphat in 2 Chronicles chapter 20. King Jehoshaphat was faced with war from three surrounding kings, and he was, scripture tells us, terrified (verse 3). Verse 12 is an incredible verse: Jehoshaphat is praying: "O our God, won't you stop them? We are powerless against this mighty army that is about to attack us. We do not know what to do, but we are looking to you for help."

Everyone was gathered together in fear: men, women, and children. God answered, "Do not be afraid! Don't be discouraged by this mighty army, for the battle is not yours, but God's" (verse 14). "Take your positions; then stand still and watch the Lord's victory" (verse 17). The king and the people all then bowed in worship.

As they went into battle, they were led by their choir. They went singing and praising the Lord. Their song? "Give thanks to the Lord; his faithful love endures forever" (verse 21). Verse 22 tells us the armies of the enemies began fighting each other and ended up destroying each other. God gave victory in the battle.

Do you need a blessing? Like Jacob, tell the Lord you will not release your hold on Him until He blesses you. Jacob was basically scared to death, at the end of his proverbial rope. His brother was coming, he was sure, with the intention of destroying him and his family. Or at least to rob him of his possessions as payback for Jacob's earlier theft of the family birthright. Jacob, filled with repentance and fear, wrestled all night in prayer. And when he found the one he was wrestling with was the Lord, he refused to let go of Him until He blessed him. And bless him, He did.

Do you have a Jericho, a problem, a concern, a situation that is surrounded by huge barriers or walls that you are powerless to bring down? You may feel there is absolutely nothing you can do about the situation. When we are faithful to God's direction and leading, He will bring down the barriers for us. And that faithfulness may be that we place all our trust in Him for the concern and the solution, and let it rest with Him. Yes, that may be all we can do. Yes, we may have to march around for seven days or seven years, or longer. But as long as we give the problem to Him, and knowing that we can do nothing about the concern, we trust Him to break down the barriers, in His time, at just the right time. Our God loves to take down barriers.

Do you have an army marching against you, a battle that you have no weapons against? You can't win? An army of danger, fear, worry? For yourself? For your children? For a health issue? Or any number of things that challenge us in today's world. If we take it to God, we realize that we are powerless and accept God's promise that the battle is not ours, but His; when we bow in loving trust and worship, when we lift our voices in a song of thanks, we can march ahead, day by day, with a heart full of joy because "His faithful love endures forever" (2 Chronicles 20:21) and our God will bring victory to this battle. Find your song.

So back to our first set of questions: Will God answer our prayers just the way we want? What do we do when our prayers don't seem to be answered? How do we respond when God seems to say, "No," or "Wait, not now"? How do we have a joyful heart when we are worried about a situation that doesn't seem to be getting any better, no matter how hard we pray? Can we have joy when we seem to be waiting and waiting?

Remember Jacob, Jericho, and Jehoshaphat. Ask God for a blessing, to remove the barriers, and to fight your battles for you. He will bring victory. It may not be in just the way you expected or at the time you wanted, but He will always do the very best if you are faithful to Him.

So remember the three Js and three Bs.

Jacob: Blessings.
Jericho: Barriers broken down.
Jehoshaphat: Battles won.

There are over thirty-five hundred promises in God's Word. Look for phrases that include "faith," "assurance," "ask," "believe," "claim," "receive," "trust," "hope," "promise," "bring my prayer," "expectantly," "confidence," "cry out," "call upon," "great things," "unlimited," "possible," "impossible," "ears and eyes open," "will answer," "delights," or "before we ask."

Expect Texts

- Numbers 23:19
- Deuteronomy 3:22
- Joshua 1:5
- 1 Samuel 12:22
- 2 Kings 6:17
- 1 Chronicles 4:10
- 2 Chronicles 6:10
- Nehemiah 1:11
- Psalm 3:4
- Psalm 38:15
- Isaiah 14:27
- Jeremiah 15:20
- Lamentations 3:56
- Ezekiel 17:24
- Joel 2:32
- Zechariah 13:9
- Malachi 1:9
- Matthew 9:22
- Mark 5:34
- Luke 7:50
- John 6:37
- Acts. 15:11
- Romans 1:17
- 1 Corinthians 1:9
- Galatians 3:29
- Ephesians 3:16
- Philippians 4:19
- 1 Thessalonians 5:24
- 2 Timothy 2:7
- Hebrews 6:19
- James 1:5
- 1 Peter 2:6
- 1 John 3:22
- Revelation 22:12

CHAPTER 6

Rejoice

Royal Blue

Express Great Joy

Finally, brethren, REJOICE, be made complete, be comforted, be like-minded, live in peace, and the God of love and peace shall be with you.
—2 Corinthians 13:11 (NASB)

What Does It Mean to Rejoice?

What words come to mind as you think of rejoicing in the Lord? My favorite is *joy*.

_____

_____

A friend once answered my question, "What is joy?" this way:

"Something happens to you that makes you very happy and gives you a lot of pleasure. Later, when you think back on it, you have a feeling; what is that feeling? That feeling is joy."

A celebration usually occurs, there is rejoicing, when victory has been declared, be it war, an examination, or any challenge in life.

Victory has been declared, the battle fought, the war won. The mighty God of the universe, by His Son Jesus, has fought the battle, paid the price, and declared victory. There is reason for joy.

So REJOICE you sons of Zion, and be glad in the Lord your God.
—Joel 2:23 (NASB)

The Lord's Prayer

The final two words of the Lord's Prayer give cause for joy: "Forever, Amen" (Matthew 6:13 KJV).

Jesus knows the victory is won, forever. We, too, may know the victory has been won for us, forever. Forever, the kingdom, the power, and the glory belong to God. There is cause for rejoicing, cause for celebration.

What Does the Bible Say?

WHAT IS THE SOURCE OF JOY?

John 15:11 _____

Romans 15:13 _____

John 17:13 _____

Psalm 4:7 _____

Nehemiah 8:10 _____

Galatians 5:22 _____

Like praise, gratitude, forgiveness, submission, and God's promises, joy is a gift.

WHAT IS THE RESULT OF JOY?

Proverbs 17:22_____

Proverbs 15:13 _____

Philippians 2:18 _____

WHO HAS CAUSE FOR REJOICING?

2 Chronicles 6:41 _____

Psalm 5:11 _____

Psalm 13:5 _____

Psalm 32:11_____

Psalm 40:16 _____

Psalm 70:4 _____

Isaiah 65:13, 14 _____

1 Peter 1:8 _____

Donna L. Bechthold

WHY DO WE REJOICE?

Psalm 31:7 _____

Psalm 33:21 _____

Psalm 63:7 _____

Psalm 118:24 _____

Psalm 126:3 _____

Isaiah 65:18 _____

Matthew 5:12 _____

Luke 1:47 _____

Luke 10:20 _____

John 16:20, 22 _____

Philippians 1:18 _____

WHEN DO WE REJOICE?

1 Thessalonians 5:16 _____

Psalm 31:7 _____

Psalm 118:24 _____

HOW DO WE REJOICE?

Psalm 9:2 _____

Psalm 13:6 _____

Psalm 32:11_____

A young evangelist once gave the following reasons for his joy:

> "There Is a Fountain Filled with Blood."
> "Jesus Loves Me, This I Know."
> "Jesus Never Fails."
> "There Is Power in the Blood."
> "My Home's in Heaven."
> "I'm a Child of the King."
> "Amazing Grace, How Sweet the Sound."
> "Our God Reigns."
> "He's Able, He's Able."
> "He Is Lord, He Is Lord."
> "It Is Well with My Soul."
> "All the Way My Savior Leads Me."
> "Because He Lives."
> "Christ the Lord Is Risen Today."
> "For God so Loved the World."
> "God Sent His Son, They Called Him Jesus."

> Glory in His holy name; let the heart of
> those who seek the Lord be glad.
> —Psalm 105:3 (NASB)

Donna L. Bechthold

My Personal Rejoicing

_____

_____

_____

_____

As you continue your study, look for phrases like these: "delight," "celebrate," "revel," "triumph," "glory," "joy," "victory," "gladness," or "cheerful face."

Rejoice Texts

➢ Deuteronomy 16:11
➢ 1 Samuel 2:1
➢ Nehemiah 12:43
➢ Psalm 1:2
➢ Psalm 21:6
➢ Psalm 40:8
➢ Psalm 85:6

➢ Ecclesiastes 5:19
➢ Isaiah 25:9
➢ Jeremiah 15:16
➢ Habakkuk 3:18
➢ Zephaniah 3:17
➢ Luke 1:14
➢ John 4:36

➢ Acts 2:28
➢ Romans 5:2
➢ 2 Corinthians 1:12
➢ Philippians 1:26
➢ 1 Thessalonians 2:19
➢ Hebrews 3:6
➢ 1 Peter 1:8

PART 2

THE SANCTUARY AND THE COLORS OF PRAYER

One of the most intriguing stories in the Bible is the story of the exodus of the children of Israel from Egypt after more than four hundred years of slavery. The story is found in the book of Exodus. It is the story of their long journey through the desert wilderness and God's interactions with and instructions to them.

They were the people God wanted to take His message to the world, the ones to prepare the world for the coming Messiah, but they didn't even know Him. Promises had been made and long forgotten by them, but not by God.

How to teach them? How to show them? How to make it real, so real they would never forget? Well, God had a problem, but God also had a plan.

The Plan

God told Moses, "Have the people of Israel build me a holy sanctuary so I can live among them" (Exodus 25:8).

The sanctuary had a special purpose for the Israelites. Even today, though the ancient practices seem strange to us, there is insight to be gained in the ongoing plan of salvation, the work of Jesus, and prayer. Let's look at the sanctuary.

The Sanctuary in the Wilderness

What Does the Bible Say?

WHERE DID MOSES GET THE PLAN FOR BUILDING THE SANCTUARY?

Exodus 25:8, 9 _____

WHERE WAS MOSES WHEN HE RECEIVED THE PLAN?

Exodus 25:40 _____

HOW DETAILED WERE THE INSTRUCTIONS?

Exodus 27:1 _____

Exodus 27:9–15 _____

(Further details can be found in Exodus chapters 25 to 40.)

WHAT WERE THE DIMENSIONS OF THE COURTYARD?

Exodus 38:9, 11, 12, 13 _____

THERE WERE TWO ITEMS LOCATED IN THE COURTYARD. NAME ONE OF THOSE ITEMS.

Exodus 27:1 and Exodus 38:1, 2 _____

WHAT WAS THE PURPOSE OF THIS ITEM?

Exodus 40:6 _____

WHAT WAS THE SECOND ITEM LOCATED IN THE COURTYARD?

Exodus 38:8 _____

WHAT WAS THE PURPOSE OF THIS ITEM?

Exodus 40:30, 31_____

HOW MANY ROOMS WERE IN THE SANCTUARY, AND WHAT WERE THEY CALLED?

Exodus 26:33 _____

WHAT ITEMS WERE IN THE FIRST ROOM, AND WHAT WAS THEIR PURPOSE?

Exodus 37:17–24 _____

Exodus 27:20, 21 _____

Exodus 40:24, 25 _____

Exodus 25:23–30 _____

Exodus 30:1–9 _____

WHAT ITEM IS INSIDE THE MOST HOLY PLACE?

Exodus 26:34 _____

WHAT WAS THE COVER OF THE ARK OF THE COVENANT CALLED?

Exodus 26:34 _____

WHAT ITEM WAS PLACED INSIDE THIS PIECE OF FURNITURE?

Exodus 25:16–22 _____

DID MOSES FOLLOW GOD'S INSTRUCTIONS?

Exodus 40:17, 19, 21, 23, 27, 32 _____

A lamb was sacrificed on the altar each day. This lamb and its spilled blood represented the future death of Jesus, the Lamb of God, for the removal and forgiveness of the sins of the people.

Daily, the guilt of the sins of the people, through the blood of the slain lamb, was transferred into the sanctuary. Read Leviticus 1:3, 4.

Once a year, the High Priest entered the Most Holy Place for a special ceremony that signified the removal of the sins that had been confessed during the year. This was called the Day of Atonement.

What Does the Bible Say?

WHERE IS THE PRESENCE OF GOD REPRESENTED IN THE SANCTUARY?

Leviticus 16:2 _____

HOW IS AARON (THE PRIEST) AND HIS FAMILY PURIFIED OF THEIR SINS?

Leviticus 16:11 _____

WHERE DOES THE PRIEST TAKE THE INCENSE?

Leviticus 16:12 _____

WHERE DOES THE CLOUD OF INCENSE GO?

Leviticus 16:13 _____

WHAT DOES THE PRIEST DO WITH SOME OF THE LAMB'S BLOOD IN THE MOST HOLY PLACE?

Leviticus 16:14 _____

WHAT IS THE SIGNIFICANCE OF THIS ANNUAL CEREMONY?

Leviticus 16:16 _____

Leviticus 16:30 _____

Leviticus 16:34 _____

Many years later, King David planned and prepared for his son, Solomon, to build the permanent temple in Jerusalem.

WHERE DID KING DAVID GET HIS PLANS?

1 Chronicles 28:11–19 _____

Jesus's Priestly Ministry

What does the ancient Hebrew sanctuary have to do with us? If, as we've seen in scripture, the sanctuary was patterned after a sanctuary in heaven, what importance does that have for the Christian world today? The book of Hebrews gives us the answer.

What does the Bible say?

IS THERE A HIGH PRIEST IN THE HEAVENLY SANCTUARY? IF YES, WHO IS IT?

Hebrews 4:14 _____

WHERE IS JESUS NOW?

Hebrews 8:1 _____

WHAT IS JESUS DOING ON BEHALF OF GOD'S PEOPLE?

Hebrews 7:25 _____

HOW OFTEN WERE THE JEWISH PRIESTS REQUIRED TO OFFER SACRIFICES FOR THEIR SINS?

Hebrews 7:27 _____

HOW OFTEN IS JESUS REQUIRED TO BE SACRIFICED FOR OUR SINS?

Hebrews 7:27 _____

The Bible tells us there is a heavenly sanctuary in which Jesus, our High Priest, is ministering for us today, before God's throne, in the Most Holy Place.

Also read Hebrews 2:17; 3:1; 5:8, 9; 6:19; 9:12.

PART 3

THROUGH THE SANCTUARY WITH THE COLORS OF PRAYER

As we look at the sanctuary and the seven items of furniture, we find a beautiful correlation with each aspect of the colors of prayer.

Station One: The Courtyard
The First Color of Prayer

Praise: Our first stop is at the curtain that surrounds the courtyard. We locate the entrance, push the curtain aside that covers the entrance, and enter the courtyard. As we enter, we ask ourselves, "Why am I here? Why am I entering into worship?" We have come to worship and to praise Him for who He is and what He is like.

Station Two: The Altar of Sacrifice
The Second Color of Prayer

Respond: As we approach the altar of sacrifice, we are struck with what this represents. There is no wood, no fire, no smoke, no sacrifice on the altar, no lambs milling about, no blood spilling on the ground. The altar is cold. The ashes have been blown away. We are overwhelmed that this represents Jesus's sacrifice for us. He took our place. He died for our sins, yours and mine. He laid His body on the wood and allowed nails to be pounded through His flesh. His blood was shed for us. And us? We are given the gift of eternal life. As we look upon this scene, our hearts are overwhelmed with a response of thankfulness for what He has done for us.

Station Three: The Laver
The Third Color of Prayer

Admit: As we move past the altar of sacrifice, we come to the laver, or wash basin. Here the priests washed their hands and feet, to be clean before entering the Holy Place. (See Exodus chapters 30 and 40.) Here we see our reflection in the bronze basin. We see our need of cleansing and forgiveness. We see that this basin represents Jesus's offer of forgiveness. We confess and repent and ask that He wash us, inside and out, and make us clean.

We now enter the first room of the sanctuary. This room is aglow with a golden, warm light that reflects and surrounds us.

Station Four: The Lampstand and the Table
The Fourth Color of Prayer

THE LAMPSTAND

Yield: As we enter this room, we approach the lampstand. This lamp is made from one solid piece of gold. The centerpiece and the branches have seven burning lamps that never go out. Jesus called Himself the Light of the world (John 8:12; 9:5). We pause and yield our heart in surrender and obedience. We ask Him to fill us with His Holy Spirit, as the oil fills the lamp, so that we may burn brightly for Him. We ask the Lord to light our way, to give us guidance and direction, to help us be the light He desires us to be (Matthew 5:14).

THE TABLE

Yield: On this table are twelve loaves of bread. Jesus called Himself the Bread of Life (John 6:48, 51). At this table, we find nourishment in God's Word. We feast on His Word. We open God's Word. We read, we listen, we learn, we study, and our desire is to obey His Word (John 6:33, 35).

We reflect for a few moments and see that yes, these first four stations all represent the work of Jesus. They have a beautiful correlation to the story of salvation and the colors of prayer: praise, responding with gratitude, admitting our sin, and yielding our lives to Him. Will the next two stations also represent Jesus's work for us?

Station Five: The Altar of Incense
The Fifth Color of Prayer

Expect: The altar of incense is placed before the veil that separates the Holy Place from the Most Holy Place (Exodus 30:7). The priest burned sweet incense on it every morning (verse 7); he burned incense on it at twilight (verse 8), a perpetual incense before the Lord. The incense offered by the priest rose up over the curtain and entered the Most Holy Place. This incense was made into a fragrant perfume (Exodus 30:34). What about this incense? Revelation 5:8 tells us, speaking of the twenty-four elders, that "each one had a harp and they were holding golden bowls full of incense, which are the prayers of the saints." So here at the altar of incense, morning and evening, we claim God's promises as we lift our concerns, our petitions, our requests to Him. We lift up our needs for ourselves and our desires for others. We claim His promises. Our requests ascend as a sweet fragrance before God's throne.

Station Six: The Ark of the Covenant
The Sixth Color of Prayer

Rejoice: Now we have the final curtain before us. This curtain separates us from the Most Holy Place. We see that the curtain has been torn from top to bottom (Matthew 27:51). Because Jesus, the Lamb of God, had been sacrificed, the daily sacrifices were no longer necessary and would have no meaning. There is no longer a barrier. We step into the Most Holy Place and into the presence of God Himself. We listen for His voice and find mercy. We quietly and reverently commune with Him and rejoice that we are welcome here and that the invitation is for us. We rejoice that we are desired, loved, and wanted. We rejoice in our time with God, in the grace He so freely offers. We rejoice that He has fought the fight for us and that He has won the victory. We rejoice because we can now safely go into the world because we have the assurance that He will be with us.

We have completed our walk through the sanctuary. The sanctuary is a complete and perfect illustration of the plan of salvation. God's original purpose in establishing the sanctuary service was to be a daily reminder to the children of Israel of the Lamb of God who was to come. It is a daily reminder to us, His children today, of the Lamb of God who did come, who died for our sins and is ministering and interceding today in the heavenly sanctuary on our behalf.

We find that the sanctuary, along with the colors of prayer, bring God's Word, the plan of salvation, and prayer together in a powerful combination, bringing purpose, hope, and the assurance of salvation.

One Final Question

As we come to the end of this study guide, this question is asked over and over again: What about all the bad things that happen to people, even people who love the Lord? What about loss due to tragic accidents, when our gut is writhing in grief, serious illnesses, death that comes too soon? What about natural disasters like earthquakes, floods, famine, tornados, where many lives are lost? Is there an answer?

As I contemplate the question, the only answer that speaks to my heart is to go back in God's Word, way back, back to the beginning, in the Garden of Eden. Yes, Adam and Eve sinned. They ate the fruit. This was not what God wanted when He created this world and His children. But eating the fruit from the tree was not the main problem. Yes, they disobeyed a simple instruction. God told them simply not to eat of the tree of the knowledge of good and evil, because if they did, they would surely die. It could have been any easy test, like, don't pick the yellow roses. You know the story; you can read it in Genesis chapter 3. Satan, in the form of a serpent, came and told them that they would not die.

Adam and Eve, instead of trusting what God had said, believed what Satan said, and that was their sin: they believed that God had lied to them. That was the big sin, before they ever ate the fruit. Eating the fruit was the result of their sin. And ever since, most of humankind has chosen to believe that God lied. But scripture tells us in Titus 1:2 and Hebrews 6:18 that it is impossible for God to lie. So who do we believe?

This distrust of God put the whole of creation, and especially humanity, into a downward spiral, even those who chose to be faithful. So we live in a world that is wracked with sin and distrust of God and His Word. And all of us, each and every one of us, are subject to the effects of the downward spiral, the effects of Satan's lie.

Can we find it within ourselves to trust God when bad things happen? Look at Job. What did he say? "Though he slay me, yet will I trust in Him" (Job 13:15 KJV).

And what about the three friends of Daniel, thrown into a blazing furnace for refusing to worship the golden idol, for worshipping God alone? What did they say? The story is in Daniel chapter 3. After they had been given a second chance to bow down, worship the idol, and avoid being thrown into the furnace, they said to the king, "O Nebuchadnezzar, we do not need to give you an answer concerning this matter. If it be so, our God whom we serve is able to deliver us from the furnace of blazing fire; and He will deliver us out of your hand, O king. But even if He does not, let it be known to you, O king, that we are not going to serve your gods or worship the golden image that you have set up" (3:16–18 NASB).

In spite of the tortuous circumstances, they chose to faithfully worship the God of creation. And we, when circumstances come to us, be it disaster, pain, incredible grief, I pray that we also will choose to still believe, trust, and worship the God of creation.

From Genesis to Revelation, the message and the challenge and the question is the same: "Who will you worship?" Our Creator God has done everything that could possibly be done. He came to this world and showed us how to live, how to love Him, how to love others. He went to the cross as the sacrificial lamb and paid for the sins of the whole world. He took the punishment that we deserve. And for each of us, if we believe what God says, and accept Jesus as our Lord and Savior, and ask Him to be Lord of our lives, scripture tells us that we may have the gift of eternal life that He offers. And our God does not lie. What an amazing God!

A MESSAGE TO YOU, FROM YOUR HEAVENLY FATHER

Dear Child,

P My child, learn of Me, I am your heavenly Father, I am your Creator, your Redeemer, your Savior. Acknowledge Me. My heart of love longs for your **PRAISE.**

R I have given you life, eternal life. I have prepared more for you than you could ask or dream. Look around and see the wonders I have created for you. I long for your **RESPONSE** of thankfulness.

A I have forgotten your sins. I have thrown them into the depths of the sea. I cannot bring them to mind. So don't be afraid to **ADMIT** your sins and ask My forgiveness. Your debt has been paid. Your punishment has been taken by My Son. When I look at you, I see His righteousness.

Y My child, give Me your heart. Follow Me. I made you. I know what is best for you. Nothing would give Me more pleasure than for you to **YIELD** your life to Me. I will not lead you astray. I promise.

E I have a storehouse of treasures in My promises. You don't **EXPECT** enough from Me. Ask Me. Believe.

R All I have promised, you may have. That is reason enough for you to **REJOICE**. My gifts are plentiful. My heart is full of love. I want to lavish that love on you. Your heart may be full of joy and gladness.

I promise. I give you My Word.

With love,
Your heavenly Father

WHAT OTHERS HAVE SAID:

Jaimy: "Enclosed find check. I wish it were a million dollars to send this seminar everywhere."

Julie: "I discovered *The Colors of Prayer* during a time of deep crisis in my life; at a time in the valley of the shadow of death. For me, *The Colors of Prayer* was a map for renewing my relationship with Christ, a beacon into green pastures, and a restoring of my soul, a wonderful blessing."

Dorothy: "I really appreciate all your help in getting me started on my Bible marking."

Jeanna: "Your *Colors of Prayer* seminar was just right. I know it was providential you came. It was a weekend like none other I've experienced."

Vicky: "I'm so thrilled to receive your book, *The Colors of Prayer*. Thank you ever so much. You are indeed God's blessing to me. I'm truly grateful to Him that He used you to satisfy my need regarding my spiritual growth, especially my personal relation with God through prayer."

Printed in the United States
By Bookmasters